In Loco Parentis

PETE MARSHALL

INDEPENDENT INNOVATIVE INTERNATIONAL

Published by Cinnamon Press
Meirion House,
Glan yr afon,
Tanygrisiau
Blaenau Ffestiniog,
Gwynedd,
LL41 3SU
www.cinnamonpress.com

The right of Pete Marshall to be identified as author of this work
has been asserted by him in accordance with the Copyright,
Designs and Patent Act, 1988. Copyright © 2013 Pete Msrshall
ISBN: 978-1-909077-15-7

British Library Cataloguing in Publication Data. A CIP record for
this book can be obtained from the British Library.

Designed and typeset by Cinnamon Press
Cover from original artwork 'neglected lonely child' by Larisa
Lofitskaya © Larisa Lofitskaya; agency: dreamstime.com
Cover design by Jan Fortune

Printed in Poland

Cinnamon Press is represented in the UK by Inpress Ltd
www.inpressbooks.co.uk and in Wales by the Welsh Books
Council www.cllc.org.uk

Acknowledgments

In Loco Parentis was first published by Outsider Publications, 1991.

About the author

Pete Marshall was born in Toxteth in 1958. He left school at 15 and has worked in various occupations ranging from soldier to social worker. His writing appears regularly in literary magazines at home and abroad. Pete has had four collections of poetry published. His first was published by the Frogmore Press in 1989. His most recent work, *Agog*, a collection of poetry set in Snowdonia was published in 2011 by Cinnamon Press. Pete is married with three kids and lives on a farm in the Conwy Valley. He has an MA in creative writing from the University of Wales, Bangor. Pete is a member of the Literature Wales's writers-on-tour scheme and currently divides his time between writing, running his holiday letting business, and running residential creative writing courses in partnership with Cinnamon Press at his smallholding.

Contents

for the rag dolls

In Loco Parentis

Sleeping In

Lying in bed,
browsing through files
which read like gothic horrors
marked confidential.
Listening to the night:
a boy's hollow head drums eerily
on the carpet next door,
a girl pleads with someone to stop,
and a haunted moon-walker
shuffles along the landing outside.
Vermin scurry in the attic,
clawing at the ceiling above me
like the imprisoned souls
of tormented children.
At night
the house shifts
under its mantle of sorrow.

Ankle socks,
pink petticoats.

Once trusting eyes
plead beneath golden curls.

A lamplit thigh,
blackberries and cream;

in sanctuary
the assaulted child

is raped again
by wandering marigold fingers.

Fairy tales;
with grim determination
and bold strokes
of lurid crayon,
she conjures Stinkhorn.
Glutinous ejaculations:
smoke, or spoor,
oozing from chimney slit
in bloated purple hood.
Windows blacked out.
Red dog in doorway.
Figurine with yellow hair,
Outside, looking in.
Phallus impudicus.
Lewd erection
in a marzipan wood.

Initiation

Welcome to the morass little victim,
now heed the advice of those
who have gone before, and understand.
Begin simply: find the pain
which brings you most pleasure,
we've found cigarette burns
and ring-pull slashes most effective.
Next, lose your marbles,
this will keep them guessing,
the rape and pillage will do the rest.

Get on the bag early;
burgle a poverty of pensioners,
ransack a confusion of chapels.
Wreck your favourite possessions.
Kill a cat, if you can stomach it,
and light a fire in your room.
Stalk the night shift,
(icy fingers'll make the women freak.)
If you get caught at Christmas
wanking into knickers
over the petrol tank of a stolen mower,
pinch the pressies from beneath the tree,
and cut the brake pipes on your guvnor's van.

Tell half of them one thing,
and the other half another. Sincerely.
Crying when you're happy
goes without saying.
Rap in a logic of vengeance,
it will make them think they're wise:
kip in a cupboard, only tell lies.
And as soon as you've settled
Run away.

Waiting

His mother's not coming;
my god, how naïve we've been,
building him up for days
with mad images of merriment
and reconciliation, until
his sallow complexion shone with
visions of turkey and crackers,
and his pale eyes glistened
like baubles on a tree.

She phoned five minutes ago,
to announce a change of plan,
she's decided to spend Christmas
with her latest man;

and the boy's by the door,
a carrier bag of tatty belongings
stowed between skinny knees,
a carefully wrapped gift
in the grip of bitten fingers,
a reflection of confusion
staring him back in the face.
His mother's not coming,
but still he sits, waiting…

"The irony is the dog was in better condition than the children."

"The child was skin and bone, his eyes were sunken and the side of his face was covered in vomit and blood. His backside was covered in sores. His body was cold and very dirty, his toe and finger nails were black and uncut."

On the balcony, which was covered in dog excrement were children's toys. In the filthy kitchen, where there was rubbish and soiled nappies, there was hardly any human food. But there was food for the couple's dog.

"Animals acting by instinct look after their young better than this."

"The children were allowed to wallow in their own excreta and that of the dogs. It is completely appalling."

"worse than animals"

Their room was littered with rubbish and clothing covered in human and dog excreta

The child was skin and bone, his eyes were sunken and the side of his face was covered in vomit and blood.

On the balcony, which was covered in dog excrement were children's toys. In the filthy kitchen where there was rubbish and soiled nappies, there was hardly any human food. But there was food for the couple's dog.

"The irony is the dog was in better condition than the children."

Dove

She pulls up.
It's hot.
Concrete saps goodness
from sunlight,
reflecting only heat.
Tenement urchins mock.
Inside, miasma;
pissed nappies,
take-aways,
and feet.

Kinetic resentment.
Amid vixen glances
she perches,
a dove amongst hawks,
on the sprung edge
of their wretched sofa.
She does not judge,
nor condemn,
nor understand.
A surfeit of compassion;
her tender nature's
been workshop honed
into grey shades
of consummate naivety.
She's Micawber's mason,
building trust.

So, with questions
open-ended as tunnels
she elucidates nothing,
bar the careless
bruising nature
of children.
Bethan's in the park.
Megan's out with Gran.
Mistaking ambivalence
for progress,
she bathes
in an ambience
of non-existent empathy,
and as they guide her
out of doors,
she hears, but doubts,
and does not pause
to countenance a scratching
from within
the chest-of-drawers.

Leatherette

Mam mutters a wife's complaint,
Dad nuts her, baronial intent
spraying snot and gore
over the lad on the leatherette.

On all fours the warren concubine
watches the box, while Dad,
howling like an old tom,
humps at her from behind;

the boy looks on in silence,
while the blood dries to a crisp scab
on his Mickey Mouse T-shirt;

he'll get in trouble in care,
for being fussy about his clothes,
and for bullying the girls.

Disclosure-

said a boy
made her kiss his thingy
asked if he did anything else
said no
told her he was a bad boy
said her brother made her kiss his thingy
too
asked what is a thingy
crying, distressed, said
she couldn't tell me
told her it was OK to tell me anything
said she couldn't say nasties
told her it was OK
said it was a secret, said she'd get
battered if she told
asked by who
said mum
told her I'd protect her
said thingies are willies
told her it was OK to talk
anxious, looked around,
asked if anyone was spying
said no
said brother's friend had put his thingy
in her willy
asked how many times
said lots of times
told her that it was not her fault, that he was
bad for doing this
said he licked her willy
too
asked her to show me where her willy was
told her it was OK, that I would never
hurt her
pointed between her legs
said good girl

Accused of murdering their
baby

cruelty and neglect

Then the couple played video
games

Did not care much if it
lived or not

        his   arms   were
broken, he had eye injuries
consistent   with   being
brutally shaken and heavy
bruising on his chest

        brain   damage,
broken   arms,   detached
retinas and a body covered
in bruises

        mother laughed as
he lay "like a rag doll" in
front of her

The   rounders   bat,   found
hidden behind a cabinet in
the baby's room, could have
been used.

"become a nuisance"

Forensic
examination revealed that
it was splintered on two
sides and a damaged piece
of hair similar to the
baby's was found on one.

"Come on you
little bastard breathe."

brain damage,
broken arms, detached
retinas and a body covered
in bruises

his arms were
broken, he had eye injuries
consistent with being
brutally shaken and heavy
bruising on his chest

Did not care much if it
Lived or not

cruelty and neglect

Then the couple played video
games

by battering it with a
rounders bat

Fuck me
she says,
legs splayed;
look at it,
look at my fanny:
come on then,
it's what you want,
fuck me.

Gently, I rearrange
her night dress,
and try
to get back
to the story;
she's seven
and loves
Peter Rabbit.

Alone

Tramp's latrine;

turds cast upon pillbox debris,
stench of piss and rot,

solitary candle's macabre dance
on forty-five years
of desperate graffiti;

this is how we found him-

head in a bin-bag womb
full of sticky oblivion,

lungs coughing puke,

eyelids fluttering
like a butterfly's terminal effort;

cold and alone.

tell me children;

chrysalis,
whale song
under blue ice,
eagle,
tall pine
in a poppy field,
bear,
snowy owl
swooping low
over moonlit meadows,
elephant,
fallow deer
mesmerized by headlights,
mole,
lone wolf
on the timber line,
mouse,
weeping willow
on a dry river bank,
canary,
albatross
soaring eternally;

they see themselves as
the lonely,
the hidden,
the hunted,
and the dispossessed;

hibernation's
sleepy whisper
calls to them all;

we must find the magic
to unravel the spell

Auction

Market Day; the punters file in,
nervous as farmers at an auction.

The livestocks' primed, thinking
that first impressions count

they bellow greetings, tumble
and turn like kittens in a cage,

offer ritual sacraments, tiny
bribes in felt-tip *(pick me, pick me.)*

Our young sow, sensing disadvantage,
tries too hard, and is hushed;

the black sheep feigns disinterest
with sullen sulking defiance.

Finally falling for a pup's sad beauty
the Vendor's gavel pounds;

disappointment settles like a shroud
over the creatures left behind,

who stare dumbly at the bumper
as their chance of freedom pulls away,

a dog is for life, it tells them,
and not just for a day.

Disclosure-

Told me Uncle Vic used to open his dressing
gown and ask her to hold onto his thingy
said he was a bad man
told me he made her kiss his thingy and suck
on it until some cream came out
told her he was a very bad man, and it was
not her fault
said it was horrible
asked if he did anything else
said he knocked her about
punched her onto the couch
licked her willy
pushed his thingy into her willy
told her this was a very bad thing to do
asked her where were mum and dad
said down the pub
asked if mum knew
said no Uncle Vic said he'd batter her and
gave her sweets not to tell

"punches delivered with
extreme force", and

could have involved him being

kicked or stamped on

hit on the back

of the head, sent tumbling
down-

stairs, and punched and

kicked.

The attack,

happened after he wet himself,

resulted in a torn liver and

bowel

caused him to

bleed to death within an
hour.

A TWO-YEAR OLD

death from internal injuries

Exorcism

.   The little girl
in the floral dress
crosses the room
to press her face,
which is puffed
with tearful exertion,
against the mirror;
she cannot see me
but knows I'm in here.

Returning to the table
she removes teddy
from between dolly's legs;
with clumsy fingers
she widens the rip
in his belly,
and slowly,
ritually,
piece by piece,
removes the stuffing,
transforming him
into a flat, shapeless,
disembowelled ghost,
which she discards
like a crumpled tissue.

Then, with her pencil
gripped like a dagger,
she scrawls viciously
again and again,
until the paper shreds
and the man with fangs
is destroyed forever.

And finally,
almost as an afterthought,
she gouges
the glass eyes
from dolly's empty head,
and leaves them
on the table,
staring into space.

This tiny starburst
of emotion
imploding
into my embrace
rips through time
and space
like a comet
wreaking havoc;
a thimble full
of such fury
would plunge
with a fiery tail
to the Earth's core.

I can feel
his awesome secret
straining against
a rib of despair
in the black hole
of his breast,
but cannot
decipher it;
supernova-
he writhes again
in his frantic bid
to escape
and be loved.

Disclosure-

crying, extremely distressed, said she
had more secrets but could not tell me
told her it was OK to tell
me
said no, trembling, very scared
told her I'd protect her
said Ronnie had put his thingy into her
willy
asked who is Ronnie
said mum's boyfriend after dad
told her he was a very nasty man, said she
was a good girl for telling me, a brave girl
said please never tell mum
asked where was mum
said in bed with Uncle Vic, but please don't
tell or he'd batter her
told her I'd keep her safe
said she didn't like Ronnie because he'd made
her bleed
asked from where
couldn't talk, hysterical, hyper-ventilating
hugged her, comforted her, told her that she
was safe
said it had hurt so much
asked what did
said Ronnie had put his thingy into her bottom
and pressed her face into the pillow to stop her
from crying out

Necromancing the Ziggurat

Necromancing the Ziggurat
at their government's pleasure,
naïve new letters of law
are bandied in subtle council
by soft spoken fools
and sentimental dreamers;

but their words reek of semen,
and rattle like the bones
in a predator's cave.
For only the elderly matrons
have tasted teardrops,
only they are the oracles of expression.

Bending double in her anti-chamber
she applies a healing balm
of hatred and blame;
but listening for revenge
hears only the cockerel crow.

Geisha

Having learnt her lessons well
she hasn't played with the blusher,
she's applied it, with the skill
and intent of a Pigalle whore.
She welcomes me with a hug
seductive as Kali's embrace,
wrapping her limbs around me
like serpents, pressing her vulva
hard into my belly
with rhythmic thrusts of her pelvis,
breathing hot and musky into my ear.

Feeling the anger and anguish rise
in my own turmoil of emotions,
I push her, too harshly, to the floor;
she glances up at me coyly,
maddening fawn eyes
pleading her innocent desire
with a Geisha's trained sensuality,
then flings herself onto the couch,
pre-Raphaelite hair a billowing pillow,
svelte arm trailing, languid
as a nymph of Victorian porn.

And she knows that I'm watching her,
but pretending not to
she moistens the pout
of her slightly parted lips
with slow, intensely erotic circles
of her tiny strawberry pink tongue.
A voice whispers beware. Beware,
the angelic little child before you now
is hot as hell;
thirteen years old and panting,
frantic as a hound in heat.

"I wish I did not have that little bastard. If I did not have the bastard I would have more money in my pocket."

She was slammed violently against a floor or wall, causing massive bruising to her head and back.

neighbours heard screams coming from the flat

head and body were covered in bruises, her leg was broken in five places, a rib was broken, and a large, weeping burn, probably caused by a cigarette lighter, had been inflicted on one hand

burn

treated

by putting nappy cream and toilet paper on it, and her broken leg by wrapping it in a wet towel

called her a
'little bitch' and once
held a knife to her throat

under water for
two minutes, locked her in
a wardrobe, ran over her
injured leg, and repeatedly
stood her against a wall
before letting her fall

mother shook her
roughly when she picked her
up, and called her a "prat"
when she vomited

she had suffered
a brain haemorrhage, and
she died when the life
support machine was
switched off

"The pair turned
night into day and gorged
themselves on their own
selfish pleasures of TV and
music without a thought,
care or attention for the
baby for whom they were
responsible."

after their arrest the couple
blamed each other

Disclosure-

told me that mum brought friends back from
the pub
asked her what happened then
said mum made her hold on to their thingies
while mum put stuff up her bottom
asked what stuff
said greasy stuff, like oil
told her they were very bad people
said then they put their thingies up mum's
willy and bottom
asked where she was
said watching
asked if they did anything to her
said promise not to tell anyone
said it was OK
I'd keep her safe
told me mum made her kiss and suck
their thingies till more cream came out
told her this was a bad thing
for mum to make her do, asked
how many men were there
said lots of men
asked her how many times did it happen
said lots of times
told her that she was very brave, that none of
it was her fault, that it was all over now
crying, hysterical,
pleading with me not to tell

.

Bruised and battered beyond control.
Torrid terminations. Boozed and bloody
miscarriages of justice. A dose of the clap.

Sex and drugs and dreary adolescent liaisons;
she tooled her way through our machine
till freedom's price suckled a flat breast.

And us? We cluck like sage Arapaho, and
plot her course with the certainty of druids.
But do nothing yet. What can we do?

Follow upstanding Caligula's lead?
Pluck it from the womby mother and dash
its brains on the Ziggurat steps?

Or simply follow the downward spiral, (maggoty
napkins, infestations of lice, terminal
botty rash, schedule one babysitters?)

Either way her dreamboats are burnt,
and she is drowned in a relentless monsoon
of degradation, shame, and despair.

And either way the girlchild returns to us;
swapped for the sanctity of madness,
or purchased by the kindness of spies.

Some say – just another spoke, torn from
the wheel of life. But sometimes I wonder,
how many more before it begins to buckle?

Play

Shall we dance Baggy Pants?
Yes of course Droopy Draws.

We drop the orphans off
at the adventure playground,

(day-glo ropes and chains
acting as childminders,)

and expect them to have fun.
But they don't. Instead,

they gather at the edge
in grainy news-reel cliques:

stooped and tired looking
like old miners on a picket,

or conspiring in gangs
like Teds around a waltzer,

or scavenging for fag-ends
like derelict evacuees.

Only two children play,
and they invent new games.

What are you doing
we ask the boy who is
burning down the wendy house?

What are the rules
we ask the girl who is
placing the dog shit on the slide?

With unconcealed contempt
they sing the same reply:

*But how can we dance if
we don't know the reason why?*

Jimbo

All you need to know
is I'm Jimbo
and I fuckin' hate you.
And I don't want to talk about it.
And I've heard it all before.
And I'm the Buck Boy,
proverbial and otherwise.
And anger is my waking emotion;
and each morning rage,
hot as lava, flows
through the channels of my mind,
until I ram eight knuckles
of love and hate
into the plywood above my bed.
And I've been there.
And my father loved me,
more often than most.
And I'm frightened of nothing,
but rope,
and the darkness of drawers.
And I'm just passing through.
And I'm the worn off novelty
of the new boy.

And I trash my room
so that the smashed mirror cuts
a jagged line through my reflection,
dissecting the word -C U N T-
on my forehead.
And I've been let down
and sharpened up.
And I'm haunted by fresh faces.
And when I sink into a relaxing bath
of womby oblivion,
to act my age with a knife,
they bring me back,
they imprison me in life.
And I behave for my own good.
And I topped him because.
And futility strikes me like a blow.
And unable to accept authority
I benefit from structure.
And I can cry wolf
while riding the crocodile.
And my mother will want me
if I'm yours.
And if you foster me I'll kill you.

a martial
arts fan broke down in the
dock as he recalled hitting
his daughter with a ruler,
plastic tubing and the flex
from an electric kettle

**50 blows to her
face, hands and body,
including a blow which
caused her brain to swell.**

by her hair and
took her upstairs where he
threw her into a bath of
cold water and began
punching her

**"He poured salt in
the bath and over the
cuts."**

died from a
combination of pain, shock
and exhaustion after at
least 50 blows

**"From the evidence, it
looks like a sustained
vicious attack."**

when she refused to
spell her name for him.

He continued beating her, using the tubing and flex because she was "stubborn."

"She was like a rag doll."

I said stop or you are going to kill her and that's when he punched my eye.

She was like a rag doll. She had no life left in her

'daddy, stop beating me.'

"He was a good father in a loving way. He just had a bad temper that he could not control."

deer daddi
pleez pleez cum bak howm
I mis yew so mutch
I woz so bad I
promis never neveg too be bad agayn
mummi sayz yew hat two go
becoz I towld on yew
iym so so sori shi
sayz shi haytes mi
becoz I towld lis abowt yew
pleez daddi pleez
cum bak hown agayn an pleez
tel mummi abowt us
iym so lownli now so
i jus wont it bak the way it wuz
jus liyk onli owr secrit
iv i telh them I liyd yew
can cum howm
i no iym a badd gurl
o daddi o daddi
iym so so sad so so sori
so so lownli
pleez o pleez o pleez
mayk it orl rit again
for giv yor bad gurl
I luv yew
pleez rite
pleez pleez cum back hown now

Ablutions

will you wash me there
no, wash yourself there
why
because you're old enough now
please
no, wash yourself there
but I don't mind
no
it's nice, Uncle Terry says...
I don't care what Uncle Terry says
he says it's OK, Uncle Terry always washes me there
it's not nice for grown men to wash little girls there
but Uncle Terry says...
it's not right
Daddy washes me there too
it's not right
why not
because
you think I'm dirty
no
yes you do, that's why you won't wash me there
it's not that
you hate me, or you'd wash me there, like Uncle Terry
I don't hate you
prove it then, go on, like Uncle Terry does
no, I think I'll get one of the ladies to finish washing you
please
no
please
no
see you hate me
no
and think I'm dirty
no
I want to go home, Uncle terry loves me, and Daddy
Sometimes

Disclosure-

may it please Your Worship and inform the
jury to share these dark secrets, whispered
by the child
before her untimely death

Sociology (traditional)

upper class	country gentry
middle class	upper middle middle lower middle
working class	respectable working ordinary working rough working
under class	unemployed disabled disadvantaged

<u>sub class</u>		
	inbred	atavistic
	simian	predatory
	pagan	malevolent
	amoral	idolatrous
	vicious	parasitic
	carnal	incestuous
	obscene	frenzied
	vacuous	debauched
	scabrous	prurient
	demented	debased
	bestial	licentious
	insatiable	despised

Men in donkey jackets
with upturned collars
step out of the lift.

Hob-nails echo loud
on the marble tiles
of Ziggurat floors.

They open the door
to a comfortable room
and step into light.

In the condensation
on the two-way mirror
one fingers the words:

'Inquisition begin;
you have looked out,
now we will look in.'